First
Facts®

Marie
Curie

PHYSICIST AND CHEMIST

by Lisa M. Bolt Simons

CAPSTONE PRESS
a capstone imprint

First Facts are published by Capstone Press,
1710 Roe Crest Drive, North Mankato, Minnesota 56003
www.mycapstone.com

Library of Congress Cataloging-in-Publication Data:
Library of Congress Cataloging-in-Publication Data is available on the Library of
Congress website.
ISBN: 978-1-5435-0643-3 (library binding) -- 978-1-5435-0649-5 (paperback) --
978-1-5435-0655-6 (ebook)
Summary: This book presents the life of Marie Curie, the scientist who discovered
radium.

Editorial Credits
Anna Butzer, editor; Bobbie Nuytten, designer;
Jo Miller, media researcher; Laura Manthe, production specialist

Photo Credits
Getty Images: Hulton Archive, cover, Jacques Boyer, 19, Popperfoto, 17; Newscom:
Ann Ronan Picture Library Heritage Images, 7, 15, Fine Art Images/Album, 9, Oxford
Science Archive Heritage Images, 21; Science Source: American Institute of Physics/
Physics Today Collection, 11; Shutterstock: Everett Historical, 5, 13

Design Elements
Shutterstock: matthew25

Printed in the United States of America.
010868S18

Table of Contents

CHAPTER 1

A Lifelong Scientist

In 1903 Marie Curie won a Nobel Prize in **Physics**. She was the first woman to do so. Eight years later she won the Nobel Prize in **Chemistry**. She's the only person to win this prize in two different sciences. These Nobel Prizes are just two of Marie's honors as a lifelong scientist.

physics—the study of matter and energy, including light, heat, electricity, and motion

chemistry—the scientific study of substances, what they are composed of, and the ways they react with each other

FACT Marie Curie was the
first person to win
the Nobel Prize twice.

CHAPTER 2

Blooming Scientist

Maria "Manya" Sklodowska was born in Warsaw, Poland, on November 7, 1867. Both of her parents were teachers. At the time, Poland was part of the Russian Empire. Maria had four older brothers and sisters. Maria's father taught her some science.

"I am among those who think that science has great beauty."

Marie Curie

Marie (far left) with her father and sisters, 1886

Maria graduated from high school when she was 15. Then she moved to Krakow, Poland, which was ruled by Austria. She **tutored** children. When she was 24, Maria moved to Paris, France. She wanted to study math and physics. She changed her name to Marie, the French spelling of Maria.

Studying in Secret

Maria went to a "Floating University" in Warsaw. It changed locations all the time because it was a secret from the Russians. It taught illegal classes such as Polish history.

tutor—to provide extra help for students outside of school

Marie at age 16

CHAPTER 3

Teacher and Researcher

A few years after Marie moved to Paris, she met Pierre Curie. He was also a scientist. They married in 1895. Marie became the head of her husband's physics **laboratory** after he got a new job. Marie and Pierre discovered **polonium** and **radium**. They are chemical elements. Marie and Pierre found radium to have healing abilities.

"It would be a beautiful thing to pass through life together hypnotized in our dreams: your dream for your country; our dream for humanity; our dream for science."

Pierre Curie to Marie Sklodowska

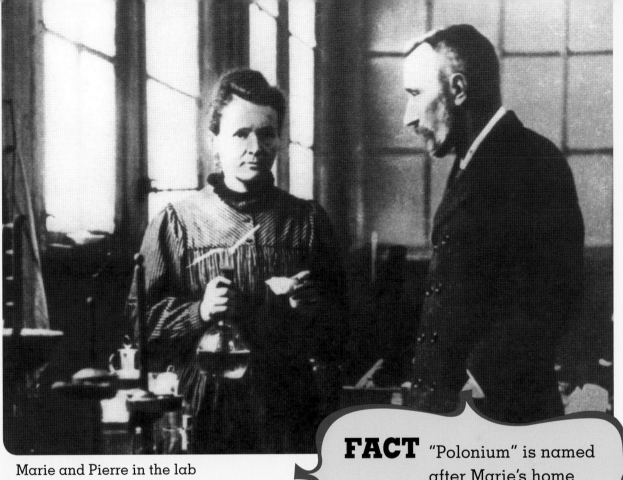
Marie and Pierre in the lab

laboratory—a place where scientists do experiments and tests

polonium—a silvery-gray element that is very radioactive

radium—a white radioactive metal element; radium can be harmful when not used correctly

11

Marie earned her Doctor of Science (PhD) degree in physics in 1903. She was the first woman in France to get this degree. The same year, she and her husband shared the Nobel Prize in Physics. The Curies also won the Davy Medal for exceptional research in chemistry. Pierre died three years later.

FACT A horse and carriage hit Pierre as he crossed a street on April 19, 1906. He died instantly.

Pierre and Marie Curie, 1903

After Pierre's death, Marie took over her husband's teaching job. It was the first time a woman taught at that university. She wrote a 971-page paper on **radioactivity** in 1910. The next year Marie won her second Nobel Prize. The prize for chemistry honored her discovery of polonium and radium.

radioactivity—a process in which atoms break apart and create a lot of energy

Marie in her laboratory, 1920

FACT In 1910 Marie could not join the French Academy of Sciences because she was a woman.

During World War I (1914–1918), Marie set up X-ray machines to help doctors who performed surgeries. Marie even put machines in ambulances and drove them to the front lines. Marie and her oldest daughter Irène also encouraged the use of radium to help soldiers in pain.

Gifted Girls

While the Curies' older daughter joined them in science, their younger daughter Ève became a journalist. She wrote a book about her mom in 1937.

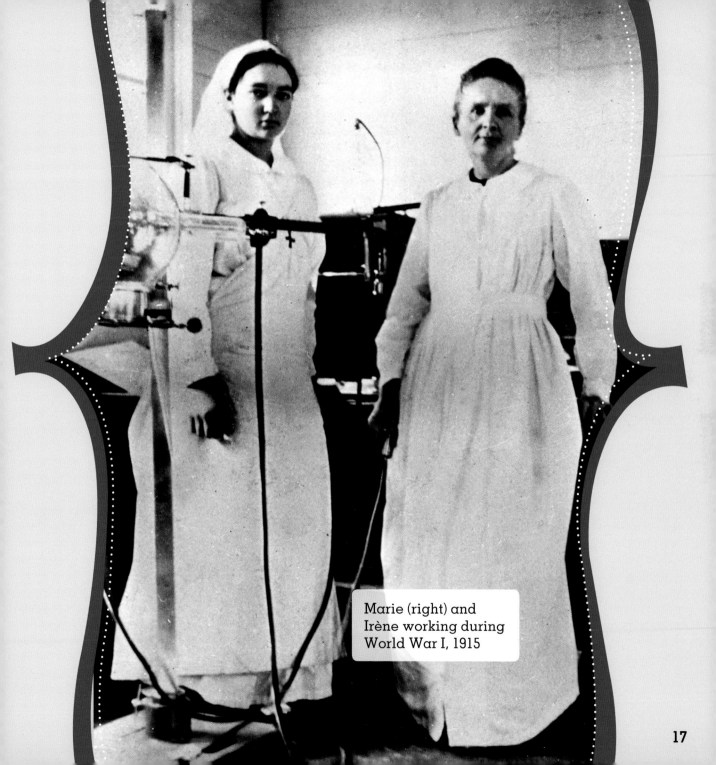

Marie (right) and
Irène working during
World War I, 1915

CHAPTER 4

Worldwide Respect

Marie was recognized for her work around the world. Colleges and universities in the United States, such as Yale University, gave her **honorary** degrees. Clubs and societies gave her honorary memberships. She published her work in science magazines. She also wrote three books on her findings.

honorary—given as a gift or in appreciation without the usual requirements

A Friendly Donation

In 1929 U.S. President Hoover awarded Marie with $50,000. The American Friends of Science donated the money. Marie used it to buy radium for her lab in Poland.

Marie speaking at the Conservatory of Arts and Crafts in Paris, France, 1925

On July 4, 1934, Marie died at age 66 of aplastic anemia. She had worked with **radiation** most of her life. It caused the disease that killed her. In 1935 Irène Curie and her husband received the Nobel Prize in Chemistry. Although they won separately, Marie and Irène are the only mother and daughter Nobel Prize winners.

"I am working in the laboratory all day long, it is all I can do: I am better off there than anywhere else."

Marie Curie

radiation—rays of energy given off by certain elements

Marie (right) and Irène, 1925

Glossary

chemistry (KE-mis-tree)—the scientific study of substances, what they are composed of, and the ways they react with each other

honorary (ON-uh-rer-ee)—given as a gift or in appreciation without the usual requirements

laboratory (LAB-ruh-tor-ee)—a place where scientists do experiments and tests

physics (FIZ-iks)—the study of matter and energy, including light, heat, electricity, and motion

polonium (puh-LOH-nee-uhm)—a silvery-gray element that is very radioactive

radiation (ray-dee-AY-shuhn)—rays of energy given off by certain elements

radioactivity (ray-dee-oh-ak-TIV-uh-tee)—a process in which atoms break apart and create a lot of energy

radium (RAY-dee-uhm)—a white radioactive metal element; radium can be harmful when not used correctly

tutor (TOO-tur)—to provide extra help for students outside of school

Read More

Avery, Lara. *Marie Curie and Her Discovery*. Science Biographies. Minneapolis, Minn.: Cantata Learning, 2015.

Edison, Erin. *Marie Curie*. Great Women in History. North Mankato, Minn.: Capstone Press, 2014.

Strand, Jennifer. *Marie Curie*. Technology Pioneers. Minneapolis, Minn.: Abdo Zoom, 2017.

Internet Sites

Use FactHound to find Internet sites related to this book.

Visit *www.facthound.com*

Just type in 9781543506433 and go!

 Check out projects, games and lots more at
www.capstonekids.com

Critical Thinking Questions

1. Why did Marie attend a "Floating University"? Why were they important at the time?

2. Do you think women still have problems getting into organizations as Marie did? Can you give any examples?

3. Why do you think the author started the book with Marie's Nobel Prizes?

Index